Cybersecurity for Small Businesses

A Practical Guide to Cybersecurity for Entrepreneurs

By

Mark David

Table of contents

Table of contents

Introduction

Why Cybersecurity Matters for Small Businesses

Small businesses are the backbone of the economy, yet they often underestimate the importance of cybersecurity. While many small business owners believe that cybercriminals only target large corporations, the reality is that small businesses are often more attractive targets. Here's why:

1. **Perceived Vulnerability**: Cybercriminals often assume that small businesses have fewer resources to invest in robust cybersecurity measures. This perception makes them a prime target for attacks.

2. **Valuable Data**: Small businesses often handle sensitive customer information, including credit card details, personal addresses, and social security numbers.

Cybercriminals can exploit this data for financial gain.

3. **Supply Chain Weakness**: Many small businesses are part of larger supply chains. By targeting a small, less-secure business, attackers can use it as a stepping stone to breach larger organizations.

4. **Reputational Damage**: A single data breach can erode customer trust and damage a small business's reputation, often beyond repair. For a small business, recovering from such reputational harm is significantly harder than for larger corporations.

5. **Financial Consequences**: Cyberattacks can be financially devastating. Costs associated with data breaches include legal fees,

regulatory fines, customer compensation, and the expense of implementing new security measures post-attack. For many small businesses, these costs can be insurmountable.

In today's digital world, cybersecurity is no longer optional. Small businesses need to adopt a proactive approach to protect their assets, customers, and reputation. Ignoring cybersecurity can lead to severe consequences that may compromise the business's survival.

Common Myths About Small Business Cybersecurity

Misconceptions about cybersecurity often leave small businesses dangerously exposed. Let's debunk some of the most common myths:

1. **"We're Too Small to Be Targeted"**
    This is one of the most pervasive myths. Cybercriminals know that small businesses often lack sophisticated defenses, making them easier targets. In fact, studies show that over **40% of cyberattacks** are directed at small businesses.

2. **"We Don't Handle Sensitive Data"**
    Many small business owners believe they aren't at risk because they don't store sensitive information. However, every business has valuable data, whether it's employee records, client information, or operational documents. Hackers can exploit even seemingly mundane data for phishing attacks or identity theft.

3. **"Our Antivirus Software is Enough"**
   While antivirus software is essential, it is far from sufficient. Modern cyber threats often bypass traditional antivirus solutions, requiring a multi-layered security approach that includes firewalls, encryption, and regular software updates.

4. **"Cybersecurity is Too Expensive"**
   Many small businesses shy away from cybersecurity due to perceived costs. However, affordable and even free tools are available that can significantly enhance security. Additionally, the cost of a data breach far outweighs the investment in preventive measures.

5. **"We're Covered by Insurance"**

Cyber insurance can provide financial protection after an attack, but it doesn't prevent an incident. Moreover, insurance policies often have strict requirements, and a lack of basic cybersecurity practices can result in denied claims.

6. **"Our Employees Know Better"**
Human error is a leading cause of cyber incidents. Even the most well-intentioned employees can fall victim to phishing scams or inadvertently compromise security. Regular training and awareness programs are crucial to minimizing this risk.

7. **"We Outsource Our IT, So We're Safe"**
While outsourcing IT services can improve efficiency, it doesn't absolve the business of

cybersecurity responsibilities. Owners must ensure that vendors follow strict security protocols and regularly assess their practices.

8. **"Cybersecurity is a One-Time Job"**
   Cybersecurity is not a "set-it-and-forget-it" task. Threats evolve constantly, and businesses must adapt by updating their systems, policies, and training to stay ahead of attackers.

Conclusion of Introduction

Understanding the importance of cybersecurity and dispelling myths is the first step toward protecting your small business. Cybersecurity is not just a technical issue but a business-critical necessity. As you navigate the digital landscape, adopting a proactive, informed approach will safeguard your assets, reputation, and long-term success. This book will guide you through practical, cost-effective strategies to build a resilient cybersecurity framework tailored to your small business needs.

Chapter 1: Understanding the Threat Landscape

Cyber threats have evolved significantly in recent years, targeting businesses of all sizes, including small enterprises. For small business owners, understanding the nature of these threats is the first step in building a robust defense. This chapter explores the types of cyber threats that small businesses face and real-life examples that illustrate the devastating effects of these attacks.

Types of Cyber Threats Facing Small Businesses

1. **Phishing Attacks**
   Phishing involves fraudulent attempts to obtain sensitive information such as login credentials or financial details by pretending to be a trustworthy entity. Attackers often use emails, text messages, or fake websites to

trick employees into divulging information.

- **Impact**: Successful phishing attacks can lead to stolen funds, compromised accounts, and data breaches.

2. **Ransomware**
   Ransomware is malware that encrypts a victim's data, rendering it inaccessible until a ransom is paid. Small businesses are frequent targets because they often lack advanced defenses.

   - **Impact**: Ransomware can halt business operations entirely, with recovery costs often exceeding the ransom demand.

3. **Malware and Spyware**
   Malware encompasses a range of malicious software, including spyware, viruses, and trojans. Spyware specifically monitors a

user's activity to collect sensitive data, often without their knowledge.

- ○ **Impact**: Malware can corrupt files, steal sensitive data, or provide hackers with remote access to systems.

4. **Insider Threats**
   Insider threats come from employees, contractors, or partners who misuse their access to company systems. These can be malicious actions or unintentional mistakes.

- ○ **Impact**: Insiders can expose sensitive data, compromise systems, or facilitate external attacks.

5. **Weak Passwords and Credential Attacks**
   Many small businesses use simple or reused passwords, making it easier for attackers to gain

unauthorized access through brute force or credential stuffing attacks.

- ○ **Impact**: Once an attacker gains access, they can exploit systems, steal data, or impersonate the business.

6. **Denial-of-Service (DoS) Attacks**

A DoS attack overwhelms a business's systems or network with traffic, causing it to crash or become unavailable.

- ○ **Impact**: These attacks can disrupt operations, damage the business's reputation, and result in lost revenue.

7. **Social Engineering**

Social engineering manipulates individuals into performing actions or divulging confidential information. These attacks often exploit human psychology rather than technical vulnerabilities.

- o **Impact**: Social engineering can lead to unauthorized access, financial loss, and reputational damage.

8. **IoT (Internet of Things) Vulnerabilities**
As small businesses adopt smart devices and IoT systems, they may inadvertently introduce security gaps if these devices are not properly secured.

- o **Impact**: Exploited IoT devices can serve as entry points for attackers or be used in larger-scale attacks like botnets.

9. **Supply Chain Attacks**
Cybercriminals target a business's suppliers or service providers to compromise the business itself. Small businesses with weaker defenses are often used as

gateways to larger targets.

- ○ **Impact**: These attacks can result in significant operational disruption and data theft.

Case Studies: Real-Life Small Business Attacks

Case Study 1: The Ransomware Attack on a Small Accounting Firm

A local accounting firm in the Midwest fell victim to a ransomware attack when an employee opened a phishing email containing malicious links. The malware encrypted all client financial records just days before the tax filing deadline. The attackers demanded $15,000 in Bitcoin.

- **Outcome**: The firm paid the ransom, but not all data was restored. They faced reputational damage, lost several clients, and incurred significant recovery costs.
- **Lesson Learned**: Regular phishing training and a robust

backup strategy could have mitigated this attack.

Case Study 2: Phishing Attack on a Small Retailer

A small online retailer received an email that appeared to be from their payment processor. The email asked for login credentials to verify a transaction. An employee unknowingly provided the credentials, granting attackers access to the company's payment gateway. The attackers made fraudulent transactions totaling $20,000.

- **Outcome**: The retailer had to reimburse customers and face legal scrutiny for not securing their payment systems.
- **Lesson Learned**: Two-factor authentication (2FA) and employee training could have prevented this breach.

Case Study 3: Insider Threat at a Small Healthcare Provider

A disgruntled former employee of a small healthcare clinic used their retained access credentials to delete critical patient records. The business had no robust offboarding process or backup system.

- **Outcome**: The clinic faced regulatory fines for failing to secure patient data and lost its reputation in the community.
- **Lesson Learned**: Implementing a strict offboarding process and access control policy would have mitigated this risk.

Case Study 4: IoT Device Exploitation in a Café

A small café implemented a smart thermostat to reduce energy costs. However, the device was connected to the same network as the point-of-sale system. Hackers exploited a vulnerability in the thermostat to gain access to customer payment data.

- **Outcome**: The café suffered a major data breach, with over 1,000 customer credit card numbers stolen.
- **Lesson Learned**: Segmenting IoT devices on a separate network and regularly updating firmware could have prevented this attack.

Conclusion of Chapter 1

Understanding the diverse types of threats and learning from real-life incidents can help small businesses adopt a proactive approach to cybersecurity. While the threats may seem overwhelming, the key takeaway is that most cyber incidents are preventable with awareness, training, and the implementation of best practices. The following chapters will delve into specific strategies to protect your small business and minimize the risk of becoming a victim of cybercrime.

Chapter 2: Building a Strong Cybersecurity Foundation

Creating a strong cybersecurity foundation is essential for protecting your small business against cyber threats. This chapter explores the importance of establishing a cybersecurity policy, the process of identifying and classifying business data, and the critical role of employee training in maintaining a secure environment.

Importance of a Cybersecurity Policy

A cybersecurity policy serves as the cornerstone of your small business's security strategy. It defines the rules, guidelines, and procedures that employees and stakeholders must follow to safeguard digital assets. Here's why it's indispensable:

1. **Establishes Clear Expectations**
   A well-drafted policy ensures that all employees understand their responsibilities regarding cybersecurity. It outlines acceptable behaviors, prohibited actions, and the consequences of non-compliance.

2. **Minimizes Human Error**
   Human error is a leading cause of cybersecurity breaches. A comprehensive policy provides guidelines for safe practices, reducing the likelihood of mistakes such as clicking on phishing links or using weak passwords.

3. **Ensures Regulatory Compliance**
   Many industries are subject to data protection regulations (e.g., GDPR, HIPAA). A cybersecurity

policy helps your business stay compliant, avoiding hefty fines and legal troubles.

4. **Supports Incident Response**
   In the event of a cyber incident, a policy provides a roadmap for responding quickly and effectively. It specifies steps to contain the breach, notify relevant parties, and recover operations.

5. **Demonstrates Professionalism**
   Customers and partners are more likely to trust a business that takes cybersecurity seriously. A formal policy showcases your commitment to protecting sensitive information.

Key Components of a Cybersecurity Policy

- **Access Control**: Guidelines for granting and revoking access to systems and data.
- **Password Management**: Requirements for creating and updating strong passwords.
- **Data Protection**: Procedures for encrypting, storing, and transmitting data securely.
- **Device Usage**: Rules for company-owned and personal devices used for work.
- **Incident Reporting**: Steps for employees to report suspicious activities or security breaches.
- **Training Requirements**: Frequency and scope of employee cybersecurity education.

Identifying and Classifying Business Data

Understanding what data your business handles and its value is critical to implementing effective security measures. Here's how to approach this process:

1. **Inventory All Data**
   Begin by listing all types of data your business collects, processes, and stores. This may include:

   - Customer information (e.g., names, addresses, payment details)
   - Employee records (e.g., social security numbers, payroll details)
   - Operational data (e.g., financial reports, supplier contracts)
   - Intellectual property (e.g., trade secrets, product designs)

2. **Classify Data by Sensitivity**
   Not all data is equally critical. Classifying data helps prioritize security measures. Common

classifications include:

- **Public Data**: Information that can be freely shared without consequences (e.g., marketing materials).
- **Internal Data**: Non-sensitive business information intended for internal use (e.g., meeting schedules).
- **Confidential Data**: Information that, if exposed, could harm the business or its stakeholders (e.g., customer details).
- **Highly Confidential Data**: Critical data that requires maximum protection (e.g., trade secrets, financial records).

3. **Determine Data Locations**
   Identify where data is stored, such as on local devices, cloud platforms, or physical servers.

Knowing the storage locations is crucial for implementing appropriate security measures.

4. **Assign Ownership and Access**
   For each data type, designate an owner responsible for its protection. Implement role-based access control (RBAC) to ensure that employees can only access data necessary for their roles.

5. **Regularly Update the Classification**
   As your business evolves, so will its data. Periodically review and update classifications to address new risks and compliance requirements.

Basics of Employee Cybersecurity Training

Employees are often the first line of defense against cyber threats. Regular training equips them with the knowledge and skills needed to recognize and respond to potential risks.

1. **Why Employee Training is Crucial**

    - **Reduces Vulnerabilities**: Employees who understand cybersecurity best practices are less likely to make costly mistakes.
    - **Encourages Vigilance**: Trained employees are more likely to recognize phishing attempts, malware, and other threats.
    - **Promotes a Security-First Culture**: Training fosters a culture where cybersecurity is a shared responsibility.

2. **Core Topics to Cover in Training**

- **Recognizing Phishing Scams**: Teach employees how to identify suspicious emails, links, and attachments.
- **Password Security**: Emphasize the importance of strong, unique passwords and the use of password managers.
- **Safe Internet Practices**: Educate on avoiding unsafe websites and downloading unverified files.
- **Device Security**: Highlight the need to lock devices when not in use and avoid public Wi-Fi without a VPN.
- **Reporting Incidents**: Ensure employees know how to report potential security breaches promptly.

3. **Delivering Effective Training**

- Use Interactive Sessions:
Engage employees with
hands-on exercises, such as
identifying phishing emails
or practicing safe browsing.
- Leverage Online Tools:
Provide access to e-learning
platforms and resources for
ongoing education.
- Simulate Real-Life
Scenarios: Conduct
phishing simulations or
role-playing exercises to test
employee responses.
- Keep It Regular: Schedule
training sessions at least
quarterly and update content
as new threats emerge.

4. Tracking and Reinforcement

- Measure Progress: Use
quizzes and assessments to
evaluate the effectiveness of
training.

- ○ **Reward Good Practices**: Recognize employees who demonstrate exceptional cybersecurity awareness.
- ○ **Provide Continuous Learning**: Share updates on emerging threats and tips through newsletters or team meetings.

Conclusion of Chapter 2

Building a strong cybersecurity foundation is essential for protecting your business from potential threats. A well-defined cybersecurity policy provides a roadmap for safe practices, while data classification ensures resources are allocated effectively to protect sensitive information. Employee training serves as a critical layer of defense, empowering your team to recognize and respond to threats. With these elements in place, your small business will be well-equipped to face the challenges of the modern digital landscape. The next chapter will focus on securing your technology and implementing practical solutions to enhance your business's cybersecurity.

Chapter 3: Securing Your Technology

A robust cybersecurity strategy begins with securing your business's technology. This chapter delves into three critical aspects: implementing best practices for password management, protecting devices such as laptops, smartphones, and IoT systems, and ensuring timely software updates and patches.

Best Practices for Password Management

Passwords are the first line of defense against unauthorized access. Weak or reused passwords are a significant vulnerability that cybercriminals frequently exploit. Effective password management can drastically reduce the risk of breaches.

1. **Create Strong Passwords**

- ○ **Length and Complexity**: Passwords should be at least 12–16 characters long and include a mix of upper and lower case letters, numbers, and special symbols.
- ○ **Avoid Predictability**: Avoid using easily guessable information, such as names, birthdays, or common words.
- ○ **Use Passphrases**: Consider using passphrases—strings of random words or phrases—for better memorability and security.

2. **Avoid Password Reuse**
Reusing passwords across multiple accounts increases the risk of credential stuffing attacks, where attackers exploit reused credentials from breaches.

3. **Leverage Password Managers**
Password managers securely store and generate unique passwords for each account. Popular tools like LastPass, Dashlane, and Bitwarden simplify password management while improving security.

4. **Enable Multi-Factor Authentication (MFA)** MFA adds an extra layer of security by requiring a second verification step, such as a code sent to a mobile device or biometric authentication.

5. **Regularly Update Passwords**
While the need to change passwords frequently has diminished with strong password policies, updating passwords after a breach or suspicious activity is essential.

6. **Monitor for Credential Leaks**
Use tools like Have I Been Pwned to check if your credentials have been compromised in data breaches. Respond promptly by changing affected passwords.

Protecting Devices: Laptops, Smartphones, and IoT Devices

Devices are gateways to sensitive business data and systems. Securing these endpoints minimizes the risk of unauthorized access or data theft.

1. **Laptops and Desktops**

   o **Use Full-Disk Encryption**: Encrypting the entire hard drive ensures data remains protected even if the device is lost or stolen.
   o **Install Security Software**: Use reputable antivirus and anti-malware

programs to detect and block threats.

- o **Enable Firewalls**: Firewalls act as a barrier between your network and potential attackers.
- o **Secure Physical Access**: Implement policies to lock devices when unattended and use cable locks for public workspaces.

2. **Smartphones and Tablets**

- o **Implement Device Locking**: Use PINs, biometric authentication (e.g., fingerprints, facial recognition), or strong passwords to lock devices.
- o **Enable Remote Wiping**: Configure devices with remote wiping capabilities to erase data if lost or stolen.
- o **Restrict App Permissions**: Only grant

necessary permissions to apps, reducing exposure to potential vulnerabilities.

- **Secure Mobile Networks**: Avoid public Wi-Fi or use a Virtual Private Network (VPN) to encrypt data transmission.

3. **Internet of Things (IoT) Devices**

- **Change Default Credentials**: IoT devices often ship with default usernames and passwords. Change these immediately upon installation.
- **Segment IoT Networks**: Separate IoT devices from critical business systems by using different network segments.
- **Update Firmware**: Regularly update device

firmware to patch security vulnerabilities.

- ○ **Disable Unnecessary Features**: Turn off features you don't use, such as remote access or voice commands, to minimize attack surfaces.

Managing Software Updates and Patches

Outdated software is a primary target for cybercriminals. Regularly updating your software ensures your systems benefit from the latest security improvements.

1. **Why Updates and Patches Matter**

   - ○ **Close Security Gaps**: Updates fix vulnerabilities that attackers could exploit.
   - ○ **Improve System Performance**: Updates

often enhance functionality and stability.

- **Ensure Compliance**: Many industries require businesses to use up-to-date software as part of regulatory compliance.

2. **Develop an Update Policy**

- **Identify Critical Systems**: Prioritize updates for systems critical to business operations.
- **Schedule Updates**: Plan updates during low-usage times to minimize disruptions.
- **Enable Automatic Updates**: Where possible, enable automatic updates for operating systems, browsers, and other applications.

3. **Patch Management Tools** Use patch management software to automate the process of

identifying, downloading, and applying patches across devices. Examples include Microsoft SCCM, Ivanti, and ManageEngine.

4. **Test Before Deploying Updates** For mission-critical systems, test updates in a controlled environment to ensure compatibility and functionality.

5. **Monitor Vendor Announcements** Stay informed about updates and vulnerabilities by subscribing to notifications from software vendors and security organizations.

6. **Update Third-Party Software** Many cyberattacks exploit vulnerabilities in third-party applications (e.g., Adobe, Java). Regularly update all installed software, not just operating

systems.

Conclusion of Chapter 3

Securing your business's technology is a critical step in building a resilient cybersecurity framework. By implementing strong password policies, protecting devices against threats, and ensuring timely software updates, you can significantly reduce your exposure to cyber risks. The measures discussed in this chapter not only protect your systems but also build customer and partner confidence in your ability to safeguard sensitive information. The next chapter will explore strategies for safeguarding networks and ensuring secure communication.

Chapter 4: Safeguarding Your Network

A secure network is the backbone of your business's cybersecurity infrastructure. Without proper protections, your network can become an entry point for cybercriminals to access sensitive data, disrupt operations, or launch further attacks. This chapter outlines essential strategies for safeguarding your network, including firewall configuration, secure Wi-Fi practices, and the use of Virtual Private Networks (VPNs).

Firewall Configuration for Small Businesses

Firewalls act as a barrier between your internal network and external threats. They monitor incoming and outgoing traffic, blocking malicious activity while allowing legitimate communications.

1. Understanding Firewalls

- **Types of Firewalls**:
  - **Hardware Firewalls**: Physical devices installed between your network and the internet.
  - **Software Firewalls**: Applications installed on individual devices to monitor and block malicious activity.
  - **Cloud-Based Firewalls**: Hosted solutions that protect cloud infrastructure and remote users.
- **Why Firewalls Matter**:
  - Prevent unauthorized access to your network.
  - Protect sensitive data from being transmitted to malicious entities.
  - Act as a first line of defense against cyberattacks.

2. Steps to Configure a Firewall

- **Set a Strong Administrator Password**: Change the default password to a complex, unique one.
- **Define Security Policies**: Identify which types of traffic to allow, block, or monitor based on your business's needs.
- **Enable Intrusion Detection and Prevention Systems (IDS/IPS)**: These features detect and block suspicious activity in real-time.
- **Block Unused Ports**: Disable any unused communication ports to reduce vulnerabilities.
- **Monitor Logs Regularly**: Review firewall logs to identify and address unusual activity.
- **Segment Your Network**: Use firewalls to separate sensitive data from less-critical systems, limiting potential damage during a breach.

3. Choosing the Right Firewall for Your Business

- For small businesses, affordable options like SonicWall, Fortinet, or Ubiquiti offer robust protection with user-friendly interfaces.
- Consider scalability if your business plans to grow, ensuring your firewall can handle increased traffic and additional features.

Secure Wi-Fi Practices

Wi-Fi networks are often targeted by hackers, particularly if they lack proper security measures. Implementing secure Wi-Fi practices is critical to protecting your business's data and operations.

1. Secure Wi-Fi Setup

- **Change Default SSID and Password**: Default network names and passwords are easy targets. Replace them with unique, complex credentials.

- **Use WPA3 Encryption**: WPA3 is the latest Wi-Fi security protocol and provides better encryption than older standards like WPA2.
- **Disable Guest Network Access**: If you must provide Wi-Fi to guests, set up a separate network isolated from your business's internal systems.
- **Reduce Signal Range**: Position your router to limit Wi-Fi signal spillage outside your premises, reducing the risk of unauthorized access.

2. Monitor Wi-Fi Activity

- Use router logs and network monitoring tools to track connected devices and identify suspicious activity.
- Disconnect unknown devices immediately and investigate further.

3. Regularly Update Firmware

- Keep your router's firmware updated to patch vulnerabilities. Many routers support automatic updates to simplify this process.

4. Implement Network Segmentation

- Divide your Wi-Fi network into segments, such as:
  - **Employee Network**: For work-related activities only.
  - **IoT Network**: Isolate IoT devices to prevent them from accessing critical systems.
  - **Guest Network**: Limit guest access to the internet only, with no connection to internal resources.

5. Educate Employees on Safe Wi-Fi Practices

- Encourage employees to avoid connecting to public Wi-Fi networks without a VPN.

- Teach them to recognize phishing attempts that exploit unsecured Wi-Fi networks.

VPNs: Do You Need One?

Virtual Private Networks (VPNs) create a secure connection between your devices and the internet, encrypting data to protect against interception.

1. Benefits of Using a VPN

- **Data Encryption**: VPNs encrypt your internet traffic, preventing hackers from intercepting sensitive information.
- **Remote Access Security**: VPNs allow employees to securely access company systems from remote locations.
- **Bypass Geographic Restrictions**: VPNs can help employees access resources that

may be restricted based on location.

- **Protect Against Public Wi-Fi Risks**: VPNs are essential when employees use public Wi-Fi, which is often unsecured.

2. Types of VPNs

- **Remote Access VPNs**: Designed for individual users connecting to a company network remotely.
- **Site-to-Site VPNs**: Connects entire office networks, ideal for businesses with multiple locations.
- **Cloud VPNs**: Secure access to cloud-based applications and resources.

3. Choosing the Right VPN for Your Business

- Look for features such as:
  - **High Encryption Standards**: AES-256 encryption is recommended.

- ○ **No-Log Policies**: Ensure the VPN provider does not store records of your activity.
  - ○ **Fast Speeds**: Select a VPN that doesn't significantly slow down internet performance.
- Popular options for small businesses include NordLayer, Perimeter 81, and Cisco AnyConnect.

4. Implementing a VPN

- Integrate the VPN with your business's existing systems and educate employees on its use.
- Establish policies requiring VPN usage for remote work and public Wi-Fi connections.

Conclusion of Chapter 4

Securing your network is a critical aspect of safeguarding your business against cyber threats. Properly configured firewalls, secure Wi-Fi practices, and the use of VPNs collectively fortify your network, making it less susceptible to breaches. By implementing these measures, you not only protect your data but also build a trustworthy reputation with customers and partners. The next chapter will explore the importance of data protection and strategies for ensuring data security within your small business.

Chapter 5: Data Protection and Backup Strategies

Data is one of the most valuable assets of any small business, making its protection a top priority. This chapter explores essential strategies for safeguarding data, including data encryption, creating an effective backup and recovery plan, and ensuring compliance with data protection laws.

Understanding Data Encryption

Encryption is a method of converting data into a coded format that is unreadable without the appropriate decryption key. It is a critical tool for protecting sensitive information from unauthorized access.

1. What Is Data Encryption?

- **Encryption Basics**: Encryption uses algorithms to scramble plaintext (readable data) into

ciphertext (coded data).
Decryption reverses the process
using a unique key.

- **Types of Encryption**:
  - **Symmetric Encryption**:
    Uses the same key for
    encryption and decryption.
    Faster but requires secure
    key sharing.
  - **Asymmetric Encryption**:
    Uses a pair of keys—public
    (for encryption) and private
    (for decryption). Ideal for
    secure communications.
  - **Hashing**: Irreversible
    encryption used for data
    integrity checks (e.g., storing
    passwords securely).

2. Where to Use Encryption in a Small Business

- **Data in Transit**: Encrypt emails,
  file transfers, and any data sent
  over networks using protocols like
  SSL/TLS.

- **Data at Rest**: Protect stored data on hard drives, servers, and cloud systems using full-disk encryption or file-level encryption.
- **Mobile Devices**: Ensure smartphones and tablets used for business are encrypted.
- **Backups**: Encrypt backup files to prevent unauthorized access if storage media is lost or stolen.

3. Tools and Techniques for Encryption

- **Encryption Tools**: Tools like VeraCrypt, BitLocker, and OpenPGP enable businesses to encrypt files, drives, and communications.
- **Cloud Encryption**: Verify that cloud service providers offer end-to-end encryption and encrypt data both at rest and in transit.
- **Encryption Policies**: Implement a business-wide encryption policy to ensure

consistent use across devices and platforms.

4. Benefits of Encryption

- Protects sensitive customer and business data.
- Mitigates risks of data breaches and leaks.
- Ensures compliance with data protection laws and industry standards.

Creating a Backup and Recovery Plan

Even with robust security measures, data loss due to hardware failure, cyberattacks, or natural disasters can occur. A comprehensive backup and recovery plan ensures your business can recover quickly and minimize disruption.

1. The Importance of Backups

- Backups protect against data loss from ransomware, accidental deletion, and system failures.
- They enable quick restoration of critical data, reducing downtime and financial losses.

2. Types of Backups

- **Full Backup**: A complete copy of all data. While time-consuming, it provides the most comprehensive protection.
- **Incremental Backup**: Only backs up changes made since the last backup, saving time and storage space.
- **Differential Backup**: Backs up changes since the last full backup, providing a middle ground between full and incremental backups.
- **Cloud Backup**: Off-site storage in the cloud, offering flexibility and accessibility from anywhere.

3. Developing a Backup Strategy

- **Define Critical Data**: Identify data essential for operations, such as customer records, financial documents, and intellectual property.
- **Schedule Regular Backups**: Automate backups to ensure they occur consistently. For critical data, consider daily or even real-time backups.
- **Follow the 3-2-1 Rule**:
  - Maintain three copies of your data (primary and two backups).
  - Store backups on two different media types (e.g., local drives and cloud).
  - Keep one backup off-site to protect against disasters.

4. Testing and Updating Your Plan

- Regularly test backups to ensure data integrity and verify recovery procedures.

- Update your plan as your business grows and data needs change.

5. Tools for Backup Management

- Small businesses can use tools like Acronis, Backblaze, and Veeam for automated backup and recovery solutions.

Compliance with Data Protection Laws

Data protection laws establish standards for handling personal and sensitive information, ensuring businesses protect privacy and security.

1. Understanding Key Data Protection Laws

- **General Data Protection Regulation (GDPR)**: Applies to businesses handling data from EU residents, emphasizing transparency, data minimization, and breach notification.

- **California Consumer Privacy Act (CCPA)**: Focuses on the rights of California residents to access, delete, and control their personal data.
- **Health Insurance Portability and Accountability Act (HIPAA)**: Governs the protection of health-related data in the U.S.
- **Payment Card Industry Data Security Standard (PCI DSS)**: Mandates security standards for businesses handling credit card transactions.

2. Key Compliance Requirements

- **Data Minimization**: Collect only the data you need and store it for as long as necessary.
- **Access Controls**: Limit access to sensitive data based on employee roles and responsibilities.
- **Data Breach Response**: Develop a plan for notifying

affected parties and regulatory bodies in case of a breach.

- **Secure Data Disposal**: Ensure data is properly erased when no longer needed, using tools like DBAN or shredders for physical media.

3. Creating a Compliance Framework

- Conduct regular risk assessments to identify vulnerabilities in data handling processes.
- Maintain detailed records of data collection, storage, and processing activities.
- Train employees on data protection requirements and ensure they understand the legal implications of non-compliance.

4. Partnering with Compliance Experts

- Hire or consult with legal and cybersecurity professionals to stay updated on evolving regulations.

- Use compliance management software like TrustArc or OneTrust to streamline efforts.

Conclusion of Chapter 5

Protecting your business's data is fundamental to building trust with customers and maintaining operational continuity. Encryption ensures data remains secure, even in the wrong hands, while a robust backup and recovery plan provides a safety net against unexpected disruptions. By adhering to data protection laws, your business not only avoids costly fines but also demonstrates a commitment to ethical data handling practices. The next chapter will focus on detecting and responding to cybersecurity incidents, equipping you to handle threats effectively.

Chapter 6: Managing Third-Party Risks

As small businesses increasingly rely on third-party vendors, service providers, and cloud-based solutions, the potential for third-party cybersecurity risks grows. A breach or failure at a vendor's end can directly impact your business. This chapter discusses best practices for managing third-party risks, including vendor vetting, understanding cloud security concerns, and contracting reliable cybersecurity services.

Vetting Vendors and Service Providers

Third-party vendors often have access to sensitive business data or systems, making it critical to ensure they adhere to robust cybersecurity standards.

1. The Importance of Vendor Vetting

- **Minimize Risk**: Assessing a vendor's security measures

reduces the likelihood of vulnerabilities affecting your business.

- **Regulatory Compliance**: Many data protection laws, such as GDPR and HIPAA, require businesses to ensure their vendors comply with security standards.
- **Protect Customer Trust**: A breach caused by a vendor can damage your reputation and customer confidence.

2. Steps for Vetting Vendors

- **Conduct a Security Assessment**:
  - Request the vendor's cybersecurity policies and incident response plans.
  - Check for certifications like ISO 27001, SOC 2, or NIST compliance, which indicate adherence to recognized security frameworks.
- **Review Their Track Record**:

- Investigate the vendor's history for breaches or security incidents.
- Look for customer reviews or references to gauge reliability and response to security issues.

- **Evaluate Access Control Practices**:
  - Ensure the vendor uses least privilege access, granting only necessary permissions to employees.
  - Verify the use of multi-factor authentication (MFA) for accessing systems.

3. Red Flags to Watch For

- Unwillingness to share security policies or certifications.
- Overly broad access to your systems or data.
- Poor incident response practices or lack of breach notification policies.

4. Ongoing Monitoring

- Periodically reassess vendor security measures, particularly when renewing contracts.
- Use automated tools like BitSight or RiskRecon to continuously monitor third-party risk levels.

Understanding Cloud Security Risks

Cloud services offer flexibility and scalability for small businesses, but they also introduce unique security challenges.

1. Common Cloud Security Risks

- **Data Breaches**: Misconfigured cloud storage or poor access controls can lead to unauthorized data exposure.
- **Account Hijacking**: Weak passwords or phishing attacks may compromise cloud accounts.

- **Shared Responsibility Misunderstanding**: Many businesses mistakenly assume cloud providers handle all aspects of security, leading to gaps in protection.

2. Shared Responsibility Model

- **Provider's Responsibility**: Physical security, infrastructure maintenance, and certain levels of encryption.
- **Your Responsibility**: Data protection, access control, and proper configuration of cloud resources.

3. Best Practices for Cloud Security

- **Choose a Reputable Provider**:
  - Opt for established providers like Amazon Web Services (AWS), Microsoft Azure, or Google Cloud, which offer advanced security features.
- **Encrypt Your Data**:

- Use end-to-end encryption for data stored in and transmitted to the cloud.
- Verify that your provider offers encryption for data at rest and in transit.
- **Implement Access Controls**:
  - Limit user access to cloud systems based on job roles.
  - Require MFA for all accounts with access to cloud resources.
- **Regularly Audit Configurations**:
  - Use tools like AWS Config or Microsoft Defender for Cloud to ensure your setup aligns with security best practices.
- **Monitor Activity**:
  - Enable logging and monitoring features to detect suspicious activities within your cloud environment.

4. Data Backup in the Cloud

- Don't rely solely on the provider's backup services. Maintain separate backups to avoid data loss during outages or attacks.

Contracting Cybersecurity Services

Outsourcing cybersecurity services can provide small businesses with access to expert protection without the need for a full-time in-house team.

1. Types of Cybersecurity Services

- **Managed Security Service Providers (MSSPs)**:
    - Offer continuous monitoring, incident response, and vulnerability management.
    - Examples: SecureWorks, AT&T Cybersecurity.
- **Penetration Testing Services**:

- Simulate cyberattacks to identify vulnerabilities in your systems.
  - Examples: Offensive Security, Rapid7.
- **Incident Response Services**:
  - Provide immediate assistance during a breach to contain and mitigate damage.
  - Examples: CrowdStrike, FireEye.
- **Compliance Management**:
  - Help businesses meet regulatory requirements through audits, documentation, and recommendations.

2. Benefits of Outsourcing Cybersecurity

- **Cost-Effective**: Access advanced tools and expertise without the expense of hiring and training an internal team.

74

- **Scalability**: Services can scale with your business's growth and changing needs.
- **24/7 Monitoring**: Continuous threat detection and response provide peace of mind.

3. Choosing the Right Cybersecurity Partner

- **Evaluate Expertise**:
  - Look for certifications such as CISSP, CISM, or CEH among the provider's staff.
- **Request Transparency**:
  - Ensure the provider clearly explains their processes, response times, and service limitations.
- **Understand Pricing**:
  - Be wary of hidden fees. Choose a provider offering straightforward pricing models.
- **Check References**:
  - Contact other businesses using the service to gauge

satisfaction and
effectiveness.

4. Creating a Service Level Agreement (SLA)

- Define clear expectations regarding:
    - Response times during incidents.
    - Specific services covered (e.g., malware removal, system monitoring).
    - Reporting frequency and format for performance metrics.
- Ensure the SLA includes provisions for terminating the contract if the provider fails to meet standards.

Conclusion of Chapter 6

Managing third-party risks is essential in today's interconnected business environment. By carefully vetting vendors, understanding the nuances of cloud security, and outsourcing cybersecurity services strategically, small businesses can significantly reduce their exposure to potential breaches. A proactive approach to third-party risk management not only safeguards sensitive data but also strengthens your business's overall cybersecurity posture. In the next chapter, we'll explore strategies for creating an effective incident response plan, enabling your business to respond swiftly and effectively to any security threats.

Chapter 7: Incident Response and Recovery

Cybersecurity incidents are no longer a question of "if" but "when." A small business must be prepared to respond swiftly and effectively to minimize damage and recover efficiently after a cyber attack. This chapter outlines the essential steps for creating an incident response plan, managing post-attack actions, and addressing reporting and legal obligations.

Creating an Incident Response Plan

An Incident Response Plan (IRP) is a structured, predefined approach to handling cybersecurity incidents. It ensures that everyone in the organization knows their role during a crisis, which reduces confusion and accelerates recovery.

1. Importance of an Incident Response Plan

- **Minimize Downtime**: A well-defined plan allows for faster containment and resolution of threats.
- **Mitigate Financial Loss**: Quick action can reduce the costs associated with data loss, operational downtime, and reputational damage.
- **Ensure Regulatory Compliance**: Many laws require organizations to respond to and report incidents within specific timeframes.

2. Key Components of an IRP

- **Preparation**:
  - Define what constitutes an incident (e.g., phishing attack, ransomware infection).
  - Establish a dedicated Incident Response Team (IRT), including IT staff,

legal advisors, and external
experts if necessary.
- Provide staff training to
ensure familiarity with the
plan.
- **Detection and Analysis**:
  - Implement monitoring tools
to detect anomalies (e.g.,
intrusion detection systems).
  - Analyze alerts to determine
the nature and severity of
the incident.
- **Containment**:
  - Decide on short-term
measures (e.g., isolating
infected systems) and
long-term strategies (e.g.,
patching vulnerabilities).
- **Eradication**:
  - Remove malware, close
breached accounts, or
disable compromised
systems to eliminate the
threat.
- **Recovery**:

- Restore systems to normal operation using clean backups.
- Test systems to ensure no residual threats remain.
- **Post-Incident Review**:
  - Document the incident and response actions.
  - Identify lessons learned and improve the IRP accordingly.

3. Building the Team

- Assign clear roles and responsibilities:
  - **Incident Coordinator**: Oversees the response effort and communicates with stakeholders.
  - **Technical Lead**: Manages technical aspects like containment and eradication.
  - **Legal Advisor**: Ensures compliance with reporting

obligations and legal
requirements.

- ○ **Public Relations (PR)
  Manager**: Handles external
  communication to manage
  reputational risks.

4. Regular Testing and Updates

- Conduct mock incident drills to
  test the plan's effectiveness.
- Update the IRP regularly to
  address new threats and
  technologies.

Steps to Take After a Cyber Attack

Responding immediately after a cyber
attack is critical to reducing its impact.
Following a structured set of actions
ensures a coordinated and efficient
response.

1. Contain the Threat

- **Isolate Affected Systems**:

- Disconnect compromised devices from the network to prevent further spread.
- Temporarily shut down affected services if necessary.
- **Preserve Evidence**:
  - Avoid altering logs, files, or settings on compromised systems to ensure evidence integrity for investigation.

2. Assess the Damage

- Identify what data or systems were affected.
- Determine the type of attack (e.g., ransomware, phishing, or denial-of-service).
- Evaluate potential business impacts, such as financial loss, reputational damage, or legal implications.

3. Notify Key Stakeholders

- **Internal Communication**:

- ○ Inform management, employees, and the IRT about the situation.
- ○ Clearly outline temporary measures or disruptions caused by the attack.
- **External Communication**:
  - ○ Notify customers, partners, or vendors if their data or services are impacted.
  - ○ Prepare a PR statement to maintain transparency and trust.

4. Recover Systems

- Use clean backups to restore affected systems.
- Ensure all vulnerabilities are patched before reconnecting to the network.
- Test systems to verify they are functioning securely and effectively.

5. Conduct a Post-Mortem Analysis

- Review logs, alerts, and other evidence to understand how the attack occurred.
- Update security measures to prevent recurrence.
- Share findings with relevant teams to improve awareness and training.

Reporting and Legal Obligations

Compliance with reporting and legal requirements is an essential aspect of incident response. Failing to meet these obligations can result in significant penalties or loss of trust.

1. Understanding Reporting Requirements

- **Regulatory Requirements**:
  - Some regulations, such as GDPR or CCPA, mandate businesses to report breaches within a specific timeframe.

- o Determine the laws applicable to your business based on your industry, location, and customer base.
- **Customer Notification**:
  - o Inform affected individuals if their data has been exposed or compromised.
  - o Provide details about what happened, the type of data affected, and steps being taken to mitigate risks.

2. Reporting to Authorities

- **Law Enforcement**:
  - o Report major breaches to local or federal law enforcement agencies, such as the FBI's Internet Crime Complaint Center (IC3) in the U.S.
  - o This can help investigate and prosecute cybercriminals.
- **Regulatory Bodies**:

- Notify agencies like data protection authorities or sector-specific regulators (e.g., HIPAA enforcers for healthcare).

3. Preparing a Comprehensive Incident Report

- Include key details such as:
  - **Timeline of Events**: When the incident occurred and how it was discovered.
  - **Scope of Impact**: Data or systems affected and potential consequences.
  - **Response Actions**: Steps taken to contain, eradicate, and recover from the incident.
  - **Future Measures**: Changes planned to prevent similar attacks.

4. Partnering with Cyber Insurance

- If you have cyber liability insurance, inform your provider about the incident.
- Collaborate with the insurer to ensure coverage for costs like recovery expenses, legal fees, and customer notifications.

Conclusion of Chapter 7

A robust incident response and recovery plan is vital for small businesses to mitigate the impact of cyber attacks. By proactively preparing an IRP, taking decisive steps during an incident, and fulfilling all legal and reporting obligations, businesses can safeguard their operations and reputation. The lessons learned from each incident also serve to strengthen future defenses, creating a more resilient cybersecurity posture.

Chapter 8: Cybersecurity on a Budget

For small businesses, implementing robust cybersecurity measures often seems like a daunting task due to budget constraints. However, financial limitations do not have to equate to inadequate protection. By leveraging free and low-cost tools, making strategic investment decisions, and tapping into community knowledge, small businesses can create an effective cybersecurity strategy without breaking the bank.

Free and Low-Cost Tools for Small Businesses

Even with a limited budget, businesses can access a variety of tools that address key cybersecurity needs. Below are some categories of essential tools and notable free or low-cost options:

1. Antivirus and Anti-Malware Software

- **Purpose**: Protect systems from malware, ransomware, and other malicious software.
- **Free Options**:
  - **Windows Defender**: Built into Windows, providing reliable real-time protection.
  - **Avast Free Antivirus**: Offers antivirus, anti-phishing, and ransomware shield.
- **Low-Cost Options**:
  - **Malwarebytes Premium**: Adds advanced threat detection and malware removal for a nominal subscription fee.

2. Password Management Tools

- **Purpose**: Generate and store strong, unique passwords securely.
- **Free Options**:
  - **Bitwarden**: Open-source password manager with secure cloud syncing.

- **Low-Cost Options**:
    - ○ **LastPass**: Premium plans with advanced sharing and family options for an affordable price.

3. Firewalls

- **Purpose**: Monitor and filter incoming and outgoing traffic to block unauthorized access.
- **Free Options**:
    - ○ **pfSense**: A free, open-source firewall solution for businesses.
    - ○ **ZoneAlarm**: Personal firewall with additional security features.
- **Low-Cost Options**:
    - ○ Hardware firewalls from companies like Ubiquiti and TP-Link, which offer enterprise-grade protection at accessible prices.

4. Virtual Private Networks (VPNs)

- **Purpose**: Secure internet connections and protect data transmission.
- **Free Options**:
  - **ProtonVPN (Free Plan)**: Offers high privacy standards without data caps.
- **Low-Cost Options**:
  - **NordVPN**: Affordable plans with high-speed servers and robust encryption.

5. Email Security and Spam Filters

- **Purpose**: Protect against phishing attacks and reduce spam.
- **Free Options**:
  - **SpamTitan**: Free trial for businesses needing robust email filtering.
- **Low-Cost Options**:
  - **Barracuda Essentials**: Provides affordable email protection and archiving.

6. Backup and Recovery Tools

- **Purpose**: Ensure data is recoverable after an incident.
- **Free Options**:
    - **Google Drive**: Free storage and basic backup capabilities (15 GB).
- **Low-Cost Options**:
    - **Backblaze**: Budget-friendly cloud backup solution with unlimited storage.

7. Education and Training Resources

- **Purpose**: Train employees on cybersecurity best practices.
- **Free Options**:
    - **KnowBe4 (Free Phishing Test)**: Assess employee vulnerability to phishing.
- **Low-Cost Options**:
    - Comprehensive online courses from platforms like Udemy or Coursera.

Prioritizing Investments in Security

When resources are limited, prioritization is crucial. Small businesses must focus on areas that provide the most significant return on investment (ROI) in terms of protection.

1. Risk Assessment

- Conduct a thorough risk assessment to identify critical vulnerabilities.
- Focus investments on assets and systems most likely to be targeted, such as customer databases or financial platforms.

2. Employee Training

- Cybersecurity awareness training is one of the most cost-effective investments.
- Educated employees are less likely to fall for phishing scams or make errors that lead to breaches.

3. Multi-Factor Authentication (MFA)

- Implement MFA to add an extra layer of protection for sensitive accounts.
- Many platforms, such as Google Workspace and Microsoft 365, offer free MFA options.

4. Backup and Recovery Solutions

- Regularly backing up critical data ensures recovery from attacks like ransomware.
- Use a combination of local and cloud backups for redundancy.

5. Managed Services

- Partner with a Managed Security Service Provider (MSSP) for affordable, outsourced security expertise.
- This allows small businesses to access enterprise-level protection without maintaining an in-house IT team.

Crowdsourcing Security Knowledge

The cybersecurity community is rich with resources, advice, and tools that small businesses can leverage. Crowdsourcing knowledge allows organizations to stay informed about emerging threats and best practices.

1. Online Communities and Forums

- Participate in cybersecurity forums like **Reddit's r/cybersecurity** or **Spiceworks**.
- Join professional groups on LinkedIn to network with experts and peers.

2. Open-Source Security Projects

- Many open-source tools, such as Snort (intrusion detection) or ClamAV (antivirus), are free and highly effective.
- Regularly check repositories like GitHub for new tools and updates.

3. Cybersecurity Newsletters and Blogs

- Subscribe to free newsletters like **Krebs on Security** or **Dark Reading**.
- Follow trusted cybersecurity blogs for timely advice and insights.

4. Local and Regional Initiatives

- Some local governments or business associations provide free or subsidized cybersecurity resources.
- Explore grants or funding programs targeted at small business security.

5. Bug Bounty Programs

- While traditionally used by larger organizations, small businesses can adapt this model.
- Reward ethical hackers for identifying vulnerabilities in your systems before malicious actors exploit them.

Conclusion of Chapter 8

Cybersecurity on a budget is not only possible but also highly achievable with the right approach. By leveraging free and low-cost tools, focusing investments on high-priority areas, and tapping into community knowledge, small businesses can create a robust cybersecurity posture. While budget constraints may limit the breadth of protections, prioritizing effectively and adopting innovative solutions can significantly reduce risk.

In the next chapter, we will discuss how to navigate legal and compliance issues to ensure your small business remains secure and compliant with relevant laws and regulations.

Appendices

The appendices provide practical resources for implementing the concepts discussed in this book. These tools will help small business owners streamline their cybersecurity efforts, ensure compliance, and safeguard their operations effectively.

1. Cybersecurity Policy Template

A well-drafted cybersecurity policy provides employees with clear guidelines for maintaining security and minimizing risks. Below is a customizable template:

Cybersecurity Policy Template

[Your Company Name] Cybersecurity Policy
Effective Date: [Insert Date]
Approved By: [Insert Name or Role]

Purpose

This policy establishes guidelines to protect [Your Company Name]'s information assets, systems, and data from cyber threats. All employees, contractors, and third-party providers must adhere to this policy.

Scope

This policy applies to:

- All employees, interns, and contractors.
- All company-owned or managed devices, systems, and networks.
- Any third-party tools, services, or platforms used by the company.

Roles and Responsibilities

1. **Employees**:
   - Follow security protocols outlined in this policy.
   - Report suspicious activity or breaches immediately to the IT team.

2. **IT Team**:
   - Ensure systems are updated and protected against threats.
   - Train employees on cybersecurity best practices.
3. **Management**:
   - Approve budgets for security tools and initiatives.

Acceptable Use

Employees must:

- Use company devices for business purposes only.
- Avoid accessing suspicious links or downloading unauthorized software.
- Store sensitive data securely using approved tools.

Password Management

- Passwords must be at least 12 characters long and include

letters, numbers, and special
characters.
- Employees must use a password
manager and enable multi-factor
authentication (MFA).

Incident Reporting

- Report all suspected breaches or
unauthorized access to [insert
contact/IT department] within 24
hours.
- Follow the Incident Response Plan
outlined by the company.

Data Protection

- Sensitive information must be
encrypted and stored in approved
locations.
- Regular backups must be
conducted by the IT team.

Policy Violations

Non-compliance with this policy may
result in disciplinary action, including
termination.

Acknowledgment

I have read and understood [Your Company Name]'s Cybersecurity Policy.

Signature:

_____

Date: _____

---

2. Checklist for Small Business Cybersecurity

Use this checklist to ensure your small business covers all critical cybersecurity areas:

General Security Measures

- Conduct a risk assessment to identify vulnerabilities.
- Establish a written cybersecurity policy.
- Train employees on basic cybersecurity practices.

Network Security

- Install and configure a firewall.

- Secure the Wi-Fi network with WPA3 encryption.
- Use a Virtual Private Network (VPN) for remote work.

Endpoint Security

- Install antivirus and anti-malware software on all devices.
- Enforce strong password policies and enable MFA.
- Regularly update operating systems, applications, and firmware.

Data Protection

- Encrypt sensitive data in storage and transmission.
- Regularly back up data using both local and cloud solutions.
- Create a data retention and disposal policy.

Access Control

- Use role-based access controls (RBAC) to limit data access.

- Disable accounts for former employees promptly.
- Monitor user activity for suspicious behavior.

Third-Party and Vendor Security

- Vet vendors for their cybersecurity practices.
- Include security requirements in vendor contracts.
- Audit vendor performance periodically.

Incident Response

- Develop and document an Incident Response Plan.
- Conduct regular drills to test response readiness.
- Establish a clear communication plan for incidents.

Budget-Friendly Tools

- Use free or low-cost security tools for antivirus, backups, and password management.

- Apply for cybersecurity grants or subsidies if available.

3. List of Recommended Tools and Resources

Here's a curated list of tools and resources to help you implement cybersecurity measures effectively:

1. Antivirus and Anti-Malware Software

- **Free**: Windows Defender, Avast Free Antivirus
- **Paid**: Malwarebytes Premium, Norton Small Business

2. Password Management

- **Free**: Bitwarden, LastPass (Free Plan)
- **Paid**: Dashlane, 1Password

3. Firewalls

- **Free**: pfSense, ZoneAlarm
- **Paid**: Cisco Meraki, Fortinet

4. Backup Solutions

- **Free**: Google Drive (15 GB), SyncBackFree
- **Paid**: Backblaze, Carbonite

5. VPNs

- **Free**: ProtonVPN (Free Plan), Windscribe
- **Paid**: NordVPN, ExpressVPN

6. Email Security

- **Free**: MailCleaner, SpamTitan (trial version)
- **Paid**: Barracuda Essentials, Mimecast

7. Employee Training

- **Free**: KnowBe4 (Phishing Test), Cybersecurity & Infrastructure Security Agency (CISA) training.
- **Paid**: SANS Institute, Udemy Cybersecurity Courses

8. Online Resources

- **News and Blogs**: Krebs on Security, Dark Reading
- **Community Forums**: Reddit (r/cybersecurity), Spiceworks
- **Government Resources**: NIST Cybersecurity Framework, Small Business Administration (SBA) Cybersecurity Tips

Conclusion of Appendices

The tools, templates, and checklists provided in this section are designed to make cybersecurity accessible and manageable for small businesses. By using these resources, you can establish a strong security foundation, protect sensitive data, and ensure resilience against cyber threats.

www.ingramcontent.com/pod-product-compliance
Lightning Source LLC
LaVergne TN
LVHW051708050326
832903LV00032B/4079